A Primary Source History of the Colony of
NEW YORK

PAUL KUPPERBERG

rosen central
Primary Source™

The Rosen Publishing Group, Inc., New York

To the citizens of my hometown. Once a New Yorker . . .

Published in 2006 by The Rosen Publishing Group, Inc.
29 East 21st Street, New York, NY 10010

Library of Congress Cataloging-in-Publication Data

Kupperberg, Paul.
A primary source history of the colony of New York / Paul Kupperberg.—1st ed.
    p. cm.—(Primary sources of the thirteen colonies and the Lost Colony)
Includes bibliographical references and index.
ISBN 1-4042-0431-8 (lib. bdg.)
ISBN 1-4042-0677-9 (pbk. bdg.)
1. New York (State)—History—Colonial period, ca. 1600–1775—Juvenile literature. 2. New York (State)—History—1775–1865—Juvenile literature.
I. Title. II. Series.
F122.K87 2006
974.7'02–dc22

2004028859

Manufactured in the United States of America

On the cover: A seventeenth-century painting entitled *Nieuw Amsterdam Ofte Nue Nieuw Yorx Oft Teylant Man* (New Amsterdam, Now New York, on the Island of Manhattan) by Dutch artist Johannes Vinckeboons. Housed in the New-York Historical Society.

CONTENTS

Introduction   The First New Yorkers   • 4

Chapter 1   Henry Hudson and the
                       Dutch West India Company   • 8

Chapter 2   Dutch New York   • 17

Chapter 3   British New York   • 31

Chapter 4   The Road to Revolution   • 40

Chapter 5   From America's First Capital
                       to America's Foremost City   • 47

                   Timeline   • 52

                   Primary Source Transcriptions   • 54

                   Glossary   • 57

                   For More Information   • 59

                   For Further Reading   • 60

                   Bibliography   • 61

                   Primary Source Image List   • 62

                   Index   • 63

INTRODUCTION

There was a time when the seat of power in New York was centered around a single tree known as the Tree of the Great Peace. The site was a gathering place for several Native American tribes and it was in the area that is now known as Syracuse, south of Lake Ontario. Of course, in those days, there was no New York State, and the borders held by various tribes were far different from those in existence today.

Humans have resided in the area that is now known as New York for more than 5,000 years. The original settlers migrated across the northern Bering Sea from modern-day Russia, traveling southeast across Canada and into the rich forests of the American Northeast. The Algonquian people first inhabited the area that would one day become the northeastern United States. They held this area for more than 300 years, spreading east to modern-day Pennsylvania and southeast to Long Island and into the Hudson River valley. The strongest of the Algonquian tribes in New York was the Muhhekunneuw, or "the people of the great [Hudson] river," who would gain fame as the Manhigan, or Mohican, people in James Fenimore Cooper's classic novel *The Last of the Mohicans* (1826).

The area around what would one day become New York City was originally occupied by three Algonquian tribal groups: the Wappinger; the Munsee and Unami Delaware; and the Metoac, which included the Manhattan, or "the people of the island." The Wappinger lived on the east side of the lower Hudson River while

The First New Yorkers

This hand-colored woodcut depicts Native American longhouses in Manhattan before the arrival of the first Dutch settlers in 1624. First settled by humans about 9,000 years ago, lower Manhattan was primarily home to the Algonquian-speaking Lenapes. These Native Americans lived throughout what would become known as New York Harbor, coastal northern New Jersey, Manhattan, Staten Island, and western Long Island. The Lenapes wandered the upper and lower bay area—which they called Lenapehoking ("place where the Lenape dwell")—throughout the year, moving seasonally. Manhattan may have served as a summer fishing camp. The trails the Lenapes made eventually formed the foundations of some of Manhattan's important streets, including Broadway.

the Delaware occupied the west side. Manhattan and Long Island belonged to the Metoac.

The strongest and most complex organization of native groups was the Iroquois League of Five Nations, established in 1570. Legend has it that Hiawatha, of the Onondaga tribe of western New York, was converted by the saintly Deganawidah, a Huron who brought a message of peace and power from the Great

Spirit. Hiawatha carried this message to his own people, as well as to the Oneida, Cayuga, Seneca, and Mohawk. They agreed to come together under a central leadership that preserved tribal autonomy and adopted a constitution, the Great Binding Law, Gayanashagowa. A joint council of fifty sachems, or chiefs, made up of representatives from each of the five tribes met every year to decide on matters of mutual concern. Other tribes had the right to join the league as well, or to "come under the Tree of the Great Peace," which was planted in Onondaga territory. Pledging not to make any hostile alliances against brother members, the league survived into the eighteenth century.

For centuries, the nations of Europe had been seeking sea routes to various points and trading ports around the globe. Most desirable was a route to the Orient, or Asia, that did not involve overland journeys of months—or even years—across treacherous terrain. There were fortunes to be made in the trade of Oriental silks, precious metals, and spices, but the difficulties and great expense of mounting overland expeditions made such travel impractical and unprofitable.

On October 12, 1492, Genoese navigator Christopher Columbus set sail under the Spanish flag on his ships the *Niña*, *Pinta*, and *Santa María* in search of a westerly route to India, which lay thousands of miles to the southeast of Spain beyond vast deserts and towering mountain ranges. Columbus never reached India, but by sailing southwest from Spain, he discovered the islands of the Bahamas, Hispaniola (present-day Haiti and the Dominican Republic), and Cuba, coming within 90 miles (145 kilometers) of the North American continent. On subsequent voyages, he ventured further south along this island chain, discovering Puerto Rico and the Leeward Islands. He also explored Venezuela, which he realized was at the northern edge of a new continent, South America.

Columbus's discoveries opened a new era of European exploration and discovery. In 1502, Amerigo Vespucci, a Florentine sailing on behalf of Spain, explored parts of the New World first found by Columbus. As a result of Vespucci's efforts, a German mapmaker named the American continents after him. Throughout the 1500s, European sea captains rode the Gulf Stream north along the east coast of North America on their return trip to Europe from all points in the partially explored Americas. It became common practice to add some last-minute profit to their voyages by stopping along the coast of North America to capture native peoples to later be sold as slaves before sailing home to Europe. For this reason, many coastal tribes became hostile to the men from across the seas. The Mahicans of the Hudson Valley lived inland, however, and had no such negative experiences with European traders and explorers. In fact, when they met their first white visitor, they were eager to exchange their valuable furs for European goods. This interest among the Mahicans attracted European traders in even greater numbers, leading to settlement, colonization, and, eventually, the loss of tribal lands.

In less than fifty years, due to increasing trade and settlement, the power in New York shifted south from the Syracuse area to a relatively small island in the New World's greatest natural harbor.

CHAPTER 1

In April 1524, the Florentine sea captain Giovanni da Verrazano ventured across the Atlantic on behalf of France, seeking a water passage to China through North America. He sailed his ship the *Dauphine*, a 100-ton caravel (a three-masted ship), into the narrow mouth of a waterway between the southwest edge of present-day Brooklyn and eastern Staten Island.

"He took a boat through the Narrows into the upper bay," writes Jan Morris in her exploration of New York City's waterways, *The Great Port: A Passage Through New York*, "and was courteously received by the Indians, who came out to meet him in their canoes, apparently wishing to act as guides, or perhaps having propositions to make about exchange rates. He saw the mouth of the Hudson—'an exceeding great stream of water'—guessed there were minerals in the hills around the Bay, took soundings, and thought the general prospect 'commodious and delightful.' 'Any laden ship,' he reported to his patron (King Francis I), could enter the harbor. A storm blew up though, da Verrazano returned to the *Dauphine*, and nobody went ashore. In the morning they were gone."

Henry Hudson and the Dutch West India Company

Hudson Sails the Hudson

It would be eighty-five more years before this great bay and the glimpsed "exceeding great stream of water" would be carefully

Henry Hudson welcomes Lenape tribesmen on board the *Half Moon* to trade for furs in this nineteenth-century painting. On September 4 and 5, 1609, Hudson's first mate, Robert Juet, wrote in his journal of two shipboard encounters with the Lenapes: "This day the people of the country came aboard . . . seeming very glad of our coming, and brought green tobacco, and gave us of it for knives and beads. They go in deer skins loose, well dressed. They have yellow copper. They desire clothes, and are very civil. They have great store of maize or Indian wheat, whereof they made good bread . . . They had red copper tobacco pipes, and other things of copper they did wear about their necks" (as quoted and transcribed by Newsday.com). A page from Hudson's journal appears above right.

explored, although Portuguese navigator Estéban Gomez would sail a short ways up what he named the Deer River in 1525, before deciding it did not lead to China and sailing back out again. It would take the Englishman Henry Hudson, seeking a northwest passage to India and sailing on behalf of the Dutch

The Colony of New York

This map was created by Adriaen Block during his 1614 expedition to North America. Block was a Dutch sea captain sent by Amsterdam merchants to establish fur trading with Native Americans in the area explored by Henry Hudson five years earlier. Block's map, which shows Manhattan, Long Island, and the southern New England coast, is the first map to accurately show Manhattan and Long Island as separate island landmasses. It is also the first map to use the term "New Netherland" to describe the new Dutch colony.

East India Company (an association of merchants from the Netherlands), to push deep into the heart of what would become New York State.

Sailing south along the North American coast in his three-masted, eighty-ton Dutch ship, the *Half Moon*, Hudson reached the lower end of present-day New York Harbor on September 2, 1609, and entered the Narrows the following day, anchoring off southwestern Brooklyn in a bay he named Gravesend. Native Americans in canoes rowed out to greet the great ship, and the two cultures engaged in peaceful trading.

A landing party was sent ashore to explore Long Island and trade with the Native Americans. Then Hudson brought the *Half Moon* to anchor off the southern tip of Manhattan Island, where they were met, according to a contemporary description quoted by Morris in *The Great Port*, by "'eight and twentie Canoes full of men, women and children . . . some in Mantles and Feathers, and some in Skinnes of divers[e] sorts of good furres.' A homely crew of Dutchmen and Britons peers down from the deck, occasionally bickering with one another, and sometimes bartering beads and knives for the Indians' tobacco leaves."

On September 12, the *Half Moon* weighed anchor. Hudson set sail north up the great river, stopping along the way at what is now Yonkers and West Point, and making it as far as present-day Albany before he determined that there was no route to India to be found there. He sailed for home, disappointed that he had failed in his mission to find the northwest passage. Hudson was entirely unaware that his one-month stay in and around New York Bay and the waterway that would one day bear his name would lead to the birth of one of the greatest cities in the history of the world.

The Dutch West India Company

Dutch explorers were lured by the promise of riches when Hudson brought back furs from the New World, and they quickly began establishing trading stations along North America's eastern seaboard. By 1610, the stretch of coast between Maine and New Jersey, as well as along the Hudson Valley, was busy with the comings and goings of fur traders from the Netherlands.

In 1613, Dutch merchants sent the *Fortuyn*, captained by German explorer Hendrick Christaensen; the *Tyger*, commanded by Adriaen Block; and three other ships to the Hudson River, or the river Mauritius, as they then called it. Block sailed down Long Island Sound, collecting and trading with the native people. He also created the first map to accurately depict Long Island as a true island and named the colony New Netherland.

Christaensen pushed up the Hudson to Albany, where he erected a crude fort, the first permanent structure built by Europeans in New York. They would also establish a fur-trading post on Manhattan, and explore and map the territory between the Delaware and Connecticut rivers, claiming it for the Netherlands before sailing home to their mother country in October 1614.

On October 11, the States General, the Dutch legislature in the nation's capital, the Hague, granted a charter and a three-year fur-trading monopoly in New Netherland to the thirteen merchants who composed the New Netherland Company. Part of the company's plan was to colonize the area, but it failed to attract colonists. As a result, when its charter expired in 1618, it was not renewed.

With both the English and the French expressing interest in gaining their own footholds in the Americas, the States General

A fleet of ships owned by the Dutch East India Company returns to Amsterdam in 1599, from a trading expedition to the Indies (present-day Southeast Asia). The ships were carrying spices, which were an extremely profitable commodity for Dutch traders. In order to create a virtual monopoly on the spice trade, the Dutch military attacked English and Portuguese trading settlements throughout the Indies. Hoping to create similar economic opportunities in the New World, in 1621, the Dutch created the Dutch West India Company closely modeled on the East India Company. It was the Dutch West India Company that founded New Netherland. To the right is an English-language copy of the Dutch document that created the Dutch West India Company.

ORDERS
AND
ARTICLES
GRANTED BY THE
HIGH AND MIGHTIE LORDS
THE STATES GENERAL OF
THE VNITED PROVINCES,

Concerning the erecting of a *VVest India* Companie:

Together with the Priuiledges and rights giuen vnto the same.

PRINTED ANNO DOM.
M.DC.XXI.

was eager to beat them to the punch and colonize the New World with Dutch settlers. On June 3, 1621, the Dutch West India Company was awarded a twenty-four-year charter for a trade monopoly by the Republic of the Netherlands. The company was organized in a similar way to the Dutch East India Company, which had held a trade monopoly for Asia since 1602. The Dutch West India Company held exclusive rights to the vast territory extending from West Africa to Newfoundland, Canada, including the Pacific Ocean and the eastern part of New Guinea.

The first permanent settlement was planned for the area first visited by Henry Hudson in 1609. "Rules for the new colony . . . were drawn up in March 1623, and a group of Walloon [French-speaking Belgians from Wallonia] families led by [Dutch explorer] Cornelius May was sent out in 1624 on the *Nieu Nederlandt*," writes George Lankevich in *American Metropolis: A History of New York City*. "The settlers were given strict instructions not to trade with foreigners and were scattered from Fort Orange [Albany], to Fort Nassau [Gloucester, New Jersey], to Nut Island [Governor's Island] in New York Bay. More settlers arrived in August 1624, and soon huts were located at Wallabout Bay on the Brooklyn shore and on the fringes of Manhattan . . . By April 22, 1625, a settlement known as New Amsterdam had been established on the southern tip of Manhattan Island."

Though the Dutch expected to profit from these trading outposts, New Netherland's two main settlements of New Amsterdam (Manhattan) and Fort Orange (Albany) were hardly vital components of the mother country's far-flung empire. Much more important and potentially lucrative to the Netherlands was

t' Fort nieuw Amsterdam op de Manhatans

This is one of the earliest known views of New Amsterdam, the primary settlement of the New Netherland colony, present-day lower Manhattan. The engraving was made in 1651, and is labeled in Dutch as *T'Fort nieuw Amsterdam op de Manhatans* (Fort New Amsterdam on Manhattan). Dutch tall ships can be seen in New York Harbor, while Lenapes paddle canoes at the mouth of the Hudson River. A walled fort, some scattered dwellings, and a Dutch windmill can be seen at the southern tip of the island. Brooklyn and Long Island are visible in the left background.

the effort to capture Brazil from the Portuguese and to establish colonies in Guiana and the West Indies. It was thought that these colonies could provide ample supplies of expensive spices and vital outposts along trade routes to Asia. The income from the fur trade in the colony of New Netherland would help finance these goals.

Though its main economic interests initially lay elsewhere, the charter of the Dutch West India Company planted the seeds of a great metropolis in the fertile soil of the New World. The small, remote, hardscrabble outpost of New Amsterdam would gradually grow in size and wealth, eventually becoming one of the world's busiest ports. Above the waters of the great bay discovered and explored by Verrazano and Hudson would one day rise a glittering, prosperous, bustling city of 8 million people, often referred to as the capital of the world.

CHAPTER 2

T he colony of New Netherland and the port of its chief settlement, New Amsterdam, became the Netherlands' foothold in the New World. The Dutch West India Company appeared to be receiving a good return on its investment when the colonists sent home furs valued at 27,000 guilders (about $10,800 today) in 1624.

In June 1625, a second company ship arrived in New Netherland with its cargo of 100 new settlers, an equal number of heads of livestock, and William Verhulst, the new director of the colony. A 1638 report from the company to the States General said, "Nothing comes from New Netherland but beaver skins, minks, and other furs," (as quoted in *A Short History of New York State*). The Dutch West India Company tried to encourage settlers to grow tobacco and produce for export.

Dutch New York

New Netherland was slow to attract new settlers to its ranks. The seventeenth century was a prosperous time for the Netherlands, and its citizens were reluctant to give up the political and economic stability and religious tolerance of the old world for the hardships, dangers, and uncertainties of the new. Competing nations were vying for a share of the fur trade—most notably England in the Connecticut Valley and Sweden in the Delaware Valley—while disputes between the Native American tribes of the Great Lakes region threatened Dutch control of the fur business at New Netherland's other chief settlement, Fort Orange, near present-day Albany.

A 1650 watercolor by Dutch artist Laurens Block depicts the growing settlement of New Amsterdam as seen from the harbor. The most prominent building visible is the Dutch Reformed Church, built between 1642 and 1643. It was the settlement's second church and was built to replace the smaller original one. At this time, New Amsterdam also included the fort, a tavern, a wharf, Dutch West India Company offices and storehouses, a barracks, a jail, a whipping post, a gallows, a windmill, and numerous houses and shops.

Despite the problems of maintaining its hold on the settlement, the Dutch West India Company continued to develop New Amsterdam. In 1626, the Dutch engineer Kryn Fredericks was sent to New Amsterdam to design a fort that would include the governor's house and the Dutch West India Company's offices. Fredericks was also to select the site for a windmill and survey roads and boweries, or farms.

Peter Minuit's $24 Bargain

New Netherland director general William Verhulst was soon replaced by a new colonial governor. Peter Minuit arrived along with 200 new settlers on May 4, 1626. The Dutch West India Company had authorized Minuit to buy Manhattan from the

Fort Orange as it would have looked circa 1635 appears in this modern-day painting by Len Tantillo. Fort Orange was the other major New Netherland settlement, along with New Amsterdam, and was designed to serve as the Dutch West India Company's headquarters in the Upper Hudson area. It was built in 1624, on the west bank of the Hudson, just south of present-day Albany, New York. It operated primarily as a fur-trading post, though soldiers were on hand to provide both protection and order, and some Dutch settlers worked beyond the fort's walls as farmers, keeping the settlement supplied with food. Settlers lived in homes built both within and nearby the fort.

native peoples, and within three weeks of his arrival, Minuit had negotiated a deal with the Canarsie Indians to purchase the 22-square-mile (57 sq. km) Manhattan Island for the bargain price of 60 guilders (calculated by a nineteenth-century historian to be about $24).

In reality, however, this bargain was too good to be true. The European settlers had no way of knowing that neither the Canarsies nor any other tribe actually owned the island and that

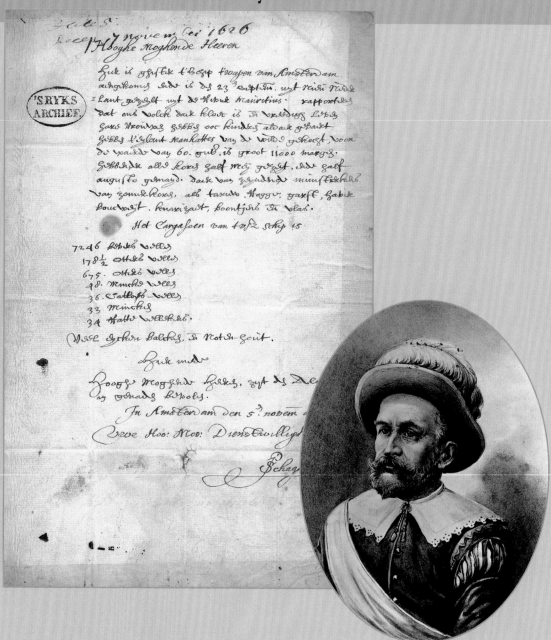

Peter Minuit, director general of New Netherland from 1626 to 1633, appears in this seventeenth-century portrait. Arriving in New Amsterdam two years after it was founded, he soon made a deal with the Canarsie Indians for the purchase of the island of Manhattan for Dutch goods. Some of the goods given to the Lenapes are thought to have included duffel cloth, kettles, axes, hoes, ceremonial and decorative beads and shells, drilling awls, and other wares. Above right is a letter from a Dutch West India Company official, Peter Schaghen, informing the company's directors in Amsterdam of Minuit's purchase of Manhattan. See a transcription of Schaghen's letter on page 54.

the deed they received in exchange for their sixty guilders was worthless. The Canarsies lived on Long Island and, along with the other area tribes, shared Manhattan as a hunting ground and a neutral trading site. Unfamiliar with European notions of land ownership and sales, the Canarsies may have thought they were simply offering hunting rights.

Still, the Dutch West India Company, feeling secure in its ownership of Manhattan, proceeded to expand beyond the protection of the fort at the southern tip of Manhattan. By 1628, the settlement's 300 residents were sending some 7,520 beaver skins a year home to the Netherlands.

While pleased with the return on their investment in the New World, the Dutch West India Company directors recognized that sending only company employees to New Netherland was too slow a way to populate the large wilderness areas they possessed. In order to encourage emigration by private individuals, the company directors adopted the Charter of Freedoms and Exemptions on June 7, 1629. In addition to establishing the first colonial government in New Netherland, the charter made an offer to any rich Dutch investors who promised to settle fifty adults in the colony within four years. Investors were given the right "to choose and take possession of as much land as they can properly cultivate and hold the same in full ownership" (as quoted in *A Short History of New York State*).

These settlements—five of which had been granted by early 1630—were owned by patroons, or Dutch landowners. All of them, with the exception of Rensselaerswyck near Albany, failed. Michael Pauw's Pavonia grant failed in 1637, but part of that grant—modern-day Staten Island—went on to become a successful partnership. Originally spelled Staaten Eylandt, it was named in honor of the Dutch parliament, known as the States General, or Staaten.

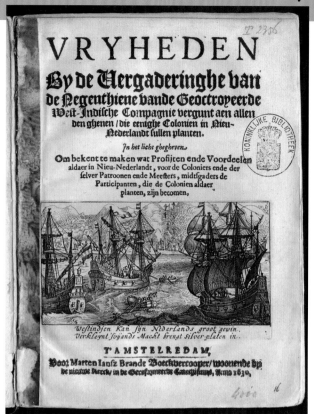

The title page of a 1630 printed copy of the Charter of Freedoms and Exemptions appears at left. The title, in Dutch, is translated as "Freedoms, as given by the council of the Nineteen of the Chartered West India Company to all those who want to establish a colony in New Netherland." The charter set up a system in which patroons—essentially landlords—could acquire large plantations, which they would rent to farmers and artisans. The Dutch West India Company hoped that this would help attract settlers and diversify New Netherland's economy, which was heavily dependent on the fur trade.

Though he would prove to be one of the more capable and honest administrators for the colony, Minuit was caught between conflicting needs and factions. His main responsibility was to the corporate interests of the Dutch West India Company. However, financial considerations were balanced against Minuit's insistence on the fair treatment of the area's indigenous people, the need to be responsive to the colonists and local merchants, and the wishes of the wealthy patroons. He was recalled to the Netherlands in 1631, on charges that he had failed to halt the illegal private trade of furs and that he favored the patroons over the colony's other inhabitants.

Under New Management

Minuit was replaced first by Bastiaen Jansen Krol, who, in only his first year as director general, quickly alienated the powerful patroons. He was soon replaced by twenty-seven-year-old Wouter Van Twiller. Under Van Twiller, the settlement of New Amsterdam and the surrounding areas saw significant growth.

The 104-soldier contingent the new director general brought with him fixed up Manhattan's deteriorating fort and built a new guardhouse and barracks. The growing town soon had its first church and minister, as well as three sawmills and a brewery. A new settlement had begun on Long Island, while across the East River, the flatlands of the Brooklyn interior were being settled and developed.

Van Twiller also signaled the company's desire to expand its influence by constructing Fort Good Hope on the Connecticut River near present-day Hartford, as well as by removing a party of Virginians who had set up camp in the abandoned Fort Nassau in New Jersey. He also stationed a garrison in the Delaware Valley to protect the company's interests in the region from such foreign powers as Sweden.

With a growing and diverse population, which included Africans and Italians, New Netherland under Van Twiller's administration was hardly the financial success the company had hoped for. In 1635, the value of exports was some 135,000 guilders ($54,000), and it seemed to many that Van Twiller was more successful at accumulating personal wealth than profits for his bosses back home in the Netherlands.

Van Twiller was replaced by Willem Kieft, who arrived on March 28, 1638, with instructions to make New Netherland a more profitable endeavor. To that end, he regulated the fur trade, taxed the colonists, and revised the patroon system. One of his most important actions was the awarding of a large land grant to a Swedish sea captain living in the Netherlands, Jonas Bronck. The captain's name remains attached to the large farm he controlled in what is now the Bronx, one of New York City's five boroughs.

Kieft became particularly unpopular with the area's native tribes. In the summer of 1640, several pigs disappeared from a Staten Island farm. Kieft blamed the theft on the Raritan Indians. Even though an investigation showed that company seamen were the true culprits, Kieft's militia killed several Indians. Relations worsened over the next two years, resulting in the Dutch massacre of hundreds of Indians and subsequent Indian retaliations that at times erupted into full-scale warfare. In a misguided attempt to protect New Amsterdam from these Indian attacks, Kieft attacked a group of Indian refugees, who had sought Dutch protection, across the Hudson in New Jersey. Eighty of them were massacred.

In all, almost 1,000 Indians and settlers were killed in skirmishes in New Netherland, until Jonas Bronck helped broker a peace with most of the warring tribes in 1642.

Bronck's efforts may have brought peace to New Amsterdam, but they did not quiet the city's internal political strife. Ignoring the advice of his own councilors, Director General Kieft decided to finance the city's reconstruction by taxing the colonists. Among the items taxed was the beer brewed and consumed by the approximately 700 colony residents, who now included Dutch, English, Brazilian, Swedish, African, German, French, Italian, Jewish, and Native American settlers. A local minister counted eighteen different languages being spoken in the city.

New Netherland's Last Dutch Leader

When Kieft opened his own brewery, he sought to boost his own profits by loosening the restrictions that he himself had earlier placed on taverns. As a result, the director general's own advisers

This 1664 plan of New Amsterdam is probably based on a 1661 map made for Dutch authorities by Jacques Cortelyou. New Amsterdam—today's lower Manhattan—is the right-hand portion of the white landmass. The sharp vertical line that forms the western boundary of the densely settled portion of Manhattan indicates the wooden wall that used to defend the city from attacks. In its place today is Wall Street, the famous thoroughfare of international finance. An illustration of the wall appears at bottom right.

petitioned the States General to recall him. There was hardly a political, religious, or business leader left in New Netherland who supported the beleaguered governor, especially in light of policies that allowed for British farming settlements in the village of Hempstead on Long Island. In the eyes of many Dutch colonists and investors, the British presence was the greatest threat facing continued company control of New Netherland.

Director General Peter Stuyvesant arrived to replace Kieft on May 11, 1647. A distinguished military man who had lost a leg in service to the company in the West Indies, Stuyvesant was both honest and intelligent. He intended to set the colony straight within three years and then move on to another assignment. As it turned out, he would govern New Netherland for seventeen years.

In addition to regulating taverns—which by the end of Kieft's directorship filled one quarter of New Amsterdam's structures—Director General Stuyvesant issued harsh penalties for smuggling. He also levied taxes on furs, wine, and liquor to pay for much-needed civic improvements. He ordered a dock built and instituted a land survey that laid out streets and building lots for new homes and businesses. In September 1647, Stuyvesant formed a nine-man board of advisers. In July 1649, the Nine, as the board was known, petitioned the States General. They claimed that Dutch West India Company mismanagement was leading to the ruin of New Amsterdam, and they called for a takeover of the entire colony of New Netherland by the national government.

The States General refused a direct takeover of New Netherland, but it did call for a restructuring of the municipal government. On February 2, 1653, Stuyvesant instituted a burgher government, appointing a ruling body of two burgomasters

Peter Stuyvesant, New Netherland's final Dutch director general, is depicted in this eighteenth-century portrait. Before being appointed director general of the colony in 1646, Stuyvesant served as the Dutch West India Company's director of the islands Aruba, Bonaire, and Curaçao. During an unsuccessful attack on the Portuguese-held island St. Martin, Stuyvesant lost his leg. The peg leg he wore afterward became a sort of trademark.

(councilmen), five schepens (aldermen), and a sheriff. This was North America's first municipal council.

Stuyvesant's seventeen-year reign, though not without conflict, left New Amsterdam a cleaner, more livable, and more efficient town than the one he had inherited from Kieft. By 1664, the city had two dozen streets and seven major paved roads crisscrossing the growing seaport. Traffic regulations were put in place, and every effort was made to enforce sanitary measures including the penning of livestock and the designation of garbage dumps for the city's more than 1,500 residents. By 1660, building codes had been enacted that were designed to lessen the risk of fire. Ample firefighting equipment, including buckets and ladders, had been acquired and fire wardens appointed to keep them in repair.

The English Are Coming!

For all its progress, however, New Netherland was living on borrowed time. Compared to the burgeoning British settlements in New England to the north and east, New Netherland's population growth was sluggish. Hundreds of English settlers already lived within the Dutch colony's borders in Connecticut, Westchester, and Long Island. As early as 1653, there were calls in the Long Island town of Flushing for English rule, while settlements along the western Connecticut waterfront on Long Island Sound agitated against Stuyvesant. A 1660 trade agreement between the Dutch director general and the English-owned Virginia colony was rejected by the English parliament, whose members were angry over the Dutch trading monopoly with the Iroquois and the Mohawks as well as New Netherland's high taxes.

Conditions between the Dutch and British settlers continued to deteriorate. Despite Stuyvesant's repeated pleas for additional troops to strengthen New Netherland during this time of heightened tension, the Dutch West India Company was unresponsive. The States General asked the English parliament to confirm the Hartford Treaty (1650), negotiated by Stuyvesant fourteen years earlier to establish a boundary between the two colonial powers on Long Island. By this time, however, the Netherlands lacked both the military might and the political will of its colonists to hold New Amsterdam.

Recognizing the Netherlands' weak grip on its American colony, England's King Charles II moved against his country's trade rival in the New World. In 1664, he granted to his brother

The 1664 surrender of New Amsterdam to English forces by Dutch director general Peter Stuyvesant is depicted in this drawing. Stuyvesant (front center, with the peg leg) and Dutch troops filed out of the fort at the southern tip of Manhattan, with neither side having fired a shot. The English allowed the Dutch to preserve their pride and dignity by letting them march out of the fort carrying their weapons, beating their drums, and flying their flags. The English would soon rename New Amsterdam as New York, after James, Duke of York and future king of England. Stuyvesant remained in the city and spent the rest of his life on his family farm, known as the "bouwerie," from which the street and neighborhood of Bowery later got their name. He died there in 1672.

James, the Duke of York and Albany, a massive tract of land on the northeastern seaboard, including "all of Maine between the Croix and Kennebec Rivers and from the coast of the Saint Lawrence, all islands between Cape Cod and the Narrows, and all land from the western boundary of Connecticut to the eastern shore of the Delaware Bay" (as quoted in *An American Metropolis: A History of New York City*). Invested with the power and authority of government and command over the residents of this vast territory, James wasted no time in securing the assistance of the New England colonies and dispatching four warships to reinforce his claims on the territory of New Amsterdam.

James's fleet dropped anchor in Gravesend Bay, in Brooklyn, on August 26, 1664. Stuyvesant was sent letters inviting his peaceful surrender, but the Dutch director general refused, tearing up the offers. The burgomasters requested a copy of the terms of surrender from the English. A petition to Stuyvesant was subsequently signed by ninety-three of New Amsterdam's leading citizens and council members, including Stuyvesant's own son, requesting him to surrender. The populace had made it clear that they were unwilling to take up arms against the invaders, forcing Stuyvesant to concede defeat.

On September 8, 1664, without a shot having been fired, Director Governor Peter Stuyvesant signed a treaty of surrender. The twenty-three Articles of the Capitulation on the Reduction of New Netherland offered the Dutch generous terms. The English granted them freedom of religion and the continuance of all property and inheritance rights. Minor civil officials were allowed to remain in office, and the citizens were guaranteed a full and free voice in all public affairs.

On October 20, Peter Stuyvesant and the rest of the citizens of the Dutch outpost took an oath of allegiance to King Charles II, and New Netherland ceased to exist. In its place, the English colony of New York had been born.

CHAPTER 3

Two years of war in Europe between England and the Netherlands followed the seizure of New York, leading to the 1667 Peace of Breda (this war is known as the second Anglo-Dutch War, and the struggle for New York was only part of a larger struggle for global dominance). The treaty allowed both sides to keep all places seized during the conflict. The Dutch were pleased to be left their dominance in the East Indies while England was content with control of North America's eastern seaboard.

Colonel Richard Nicolls was appointed the first English governor of New York, ruling in the name James, the Duke of York, for whom the colony and city were renamed. James instructed the new governor to treat the people "with humanity and gentleness" (as quoted in *A Short History of New York State*). Ruling with a light hand and allowing the established inhabitants to retain their dignity as well as property and other rights, he proved a popular governor, eventually even befriending the ousted Stuyvesant. Under the generous terms of their new colonial masters, only a few Dutch residents accepted the free passage home to the Netherlands offered by the English conquerors when they took over the colony.

British New York

British Rule

Nicolls was a benevolent governor, proving popular with New York's Dutch majority while not alienating the more heavily British towns on Long Island. He encouraged construction and expansion on Manhattan and, on March 1, 1665, issued the Duke's Laws, a series of civil and criminal laws based on the New

ARTYKELEN,

Van 't overgaen van

NIEUW-NEDERLANDT.

Op den 27. Augusti, Oude-Stijl, Anno 1664.

SYmon Gilde van Rarop, Schipper op 't Schip de Gideon, komende van de Menates, of Nieuw-Amsterdam in Nieuw-Nederlandt, rapporteert dat Nieuw-Nederlandt, met accoort, sonder eenighe tegenweer, den 8. September Nieuwe-Stijl, aen de Engelsen is overgegeven, op Conditien als volght:

Was onderteeckent

J. d. Decker.
N. Verlet.
Sam. Megapolensis.
Cornelis Steenwijck.
O. Stevensz. Cortlant.
Jacque Couseau.

Robbert Carr.
George Cartwright.
John Winthrop.
Sam. Willes.
Tho. Clarcks.
John Phinchon.

Ick stae dese Artijkelen toe *(en geteeckent)*

RICHARDT NICOLLS.

The Dutch director general of New Netherland, Peter Stuyvesant, initially resisted the terms of surrender offered to him by English colonel Richard Nicolls, whose four warships had entered the lower Hudson River in late August 1664. Stuyvesant is said to have torn up the original document that contained Nicoll's terms of surrender, vowing to be carried out of New Amsterdam dead before he would give in to the English. Some Dutch citizens pieced the document back together, however, and convinced him to read and accept the truce. A copy of the document appears above. See transcription on page 54.

England legal model. The Duke's Laws also called for a new system of local government and the establishment of a provincial court system and militia.

In June, Nicolls appointed fellow Englishman Thomas Willett to serve as New York's first mayor but awarded lesser offices to powerful Dutch burghers, granting them power as long as they operated under England's rules. During Nicolls's tenure, the shape of New York literally changed as the king took the New Jersey territory from the Duke of York and assigned it to new proprietors. On its eastern end, New York shrunk still more as it lost its claim to the Connecticut River and, in 1667, to all of Connecticut when Nicolls returned the lands lying to the east of Mamaroneck.

Francis Lovelace succeeded Nicolls as governor in March 1668. Lovelace concentrated his administration on the expansion of inhabited territory, sending settlements into the northern Bronx, which, in 1673, became the town of Fordham. He also purchased additional lands from the area's native tribes and secured the title to Staten Island, an area that had long been the subject of heavily disputed claims between New York and New Jersey.

A Brief Change in Governance

Lovelace's rule also saw the establishment of ferry service between Manhattan and New Jersey, as well as to remote towns in the Bronx. A wagon road to the town of Harlem in northern Manhattan was also built. New York's busy port grew even busier with increased trade and, until early 1672, the colony's potential appeared to be unlimited.

Then word came that the peace between the Netherlands and England had been shattered, and the two nations were again at war. Despite increasing the city's defenses, Lovelace could not keep out the Dutch fleet that appeared in New York Harbor on

Built in 1641 to 1642, the former City Tavern building of New Amsterdam appears in this nineteenth-century lithograph. In 1654, under the rule of Peter Stuyvesant, the tavern was renovated and became the town hall, or Stadthuys. The New Amsterdam city magistrates held meetings here on Mondays, between 9 AM and noon. After the English takeover of the city, the building continued to serve as New York's town hall until 1699. It stood on the corner of Pearl Street at Coentijs Slip (present-day Coenties Slip) on the East River, within the walls of the Dutch fort. Today, a small waterfront park sits on the former site of the Stadthuys.

August 8, 1673. Once again without a struggle, the colony found itself under a new master and was again named New Netherland, while the city became New Orange.

The Dutch reoccupation of New York was short-lived, however. Following the Treaty of Westminster, signed on February 6, 1674, New York was returned to English hands, and the Dutch gave up all claims to North America.

Following this brief period of turmoil, Governor Lovelace was replaced by Major Edmund Andros. While Andros failed in his attempt to convince James, Duke of York, to allow the establishment of an elected provincial assembly, he was successful in such civic projects as building an insane asylum, improving the city's wells, installing the first street lamps, and constructing a great commercial dock at the foot of Whitehall Street. New York Harbor was declared the colony's sole port of entry for imports. The Bolting Act, enacted by Andros on January 7, 1680, ordered that all grain for export from the colony of New York come through the main city for grinding, processing, and packing. Thanks in large part to this one act, New York City's wealth nearly tripled by the end of the seventeenth century.

Thomas Dongan followed Andros as governor on January 27, 1683. With the success of the Bolting Act, James had become convinced that allowing the colonists more self-government might induce them to work more effectively, so Dongan arrived in New York with instructions from the duke to create an elected assembly.

New York's First Elections

In the fall of 1683, the first provincial elections in the history of New York were held. All free men of property were allowed to vote for the General Assembly. Seventeen men from ten counties were elected and met in Manhattan on October 27. They were empowered, subject to the governor's approval, to pass laws and impose taxes. Among the first orders of business was the passage of the Charter of Liberties and Privileges, a document approved by Dongan and Duke James, that provided colonists with self-government, self-taxation, trial by jury, and a host of other rights enjoyed by the citizens of England.

In December 1683, New York was designated a provincial capital and received a new municipal charter, which divided the city into six wards, or political districts. Each ward elected an assistant and an alderman. Together with the mayor, these officials formed the Common Council, empowered to enact laws in accordance with English law. The governor retained the right to appoint the mayor and other city officials.

New York was prospering under the system established by James, the Duke of York. But when, on February 6, 1685, King Charles II died and Duke James became King James II, everything changed. At the advice of his lords of trade, James revoked the Charter of Liberties and Privileges and imposed strict imperial trade regulations on the newly consolidated Dominion of New England, which joined New York, New Jersey, and all of New England into a single colonial unit. This was done largely to create a bastion against growing French influence in the New World. Edmund Andros was called out of retirement to oversee the dominion.

A Period of Turbulence and Growing Self-Rule

King James's policies led to resentment both at home and abroad. The abolition of the charter and a free assembly outraged New Yorkers. Those outside the city resented the Bolting Act and New York's resulting flour monopoly, while merchants on Long Island bristled at the regulations that sent all trade to New York, ruining their business with Boston and the West Indies.

Resentment against James grew until, in 1688, England erupted in a civil war that led to the king's dethroning. James, a Catholic, was replaced with the Protestant monarchs, William and Mary. Governor Andros was arrested and imprisoned in Boston, while New York broke out in open rebellion.

Despite this period of chaos, New York once again settled into growth and prosperity. By 1700, the city was home to some 5,000 people from all walks of life. Its port, which remained the

William and Mary, king and queen of England, sit enthroned before a large crowd of English subjects. Mary was the Protestant daughter of Catholic king James II. She was married to her first cousin William, a Dutch prince who was twelve years older, in order to strengthen an alliance with the Netherlands. Over time, however, they were said to have developed a deep love and respect for each other.

dominant port of the New World, saw record revenues even under a series of incompetent and corrupt colonial governors. With Parliament ruling some 3,000 miles (4,800 km) away in England, New Yorkers gradually became accustomed to a form of self-rule, even if at the pleasure of the royal governor. They found it easy enough to sidestep a variety of harmful tariffs and taxes placed on various goods by the English parliament. For example, New York colonists often resorted to smuggling goods or bribing local customs officials.

The Stamp Act of 1765

Following a war with France during which time the colonies had been largely ignored and left to govern themselves, the British crown began taking measures to collect taxes to pay for the colony's upkeep and defense. As a result, colonists began to fear a greater British military presence on their shores and more government intervention in their lives. Sure enough, in 1765, Parliament passed the Stamp Act, a tax set to go into effect on November 1, on forty-three ordinary necessities of life, including marriage licenses, deeds, playing cards, and newspapers.

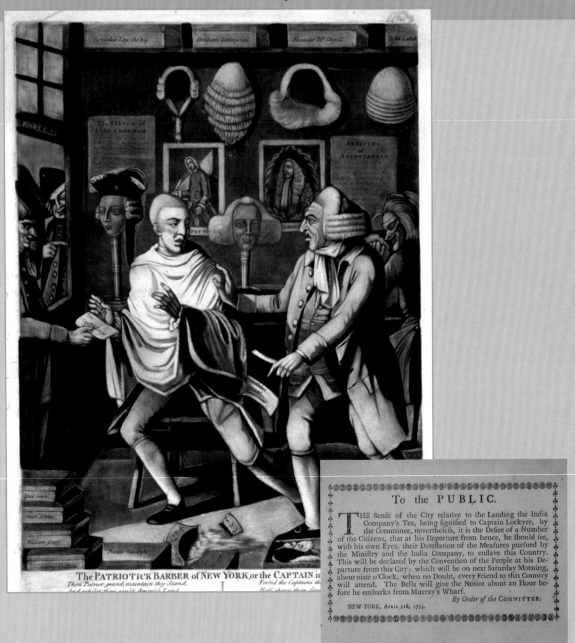

The PATRIOTICK BARBER of NEW YORK, or the CAPTAIN in

To the PUBLIC.

THE Sense of the City relative to the Landing the India Company's Tea, being signified to Captain Lockyer, by the Committee, nevertheless, it is the Desire of a Number of the Citizens, that at his Departure from hence, he should see, with his own Eyes, their Detestation of the Measures pursued by the Ministry and the India Company, to enslave this Country. This will be declared by the Convention of the People at his Departure from this City; which will be on next Saturday Morning, about nine o'Clock, when no Doubt, every Friend to this Country will attend. The Bells will give the Notice about an Hour before he embarks from Murray's Wharf.

By Order of the COMMITTEE.

NEW-YORK, APRIL 21st, 1774.

A 1775 political cartoon (*top left*) humorously reveals the growing tension in New York between the increasingly rebellious colonists and the Loyalists and British soldiers in their midst. It shows a New York barber refusing to shave a customer once he realizes the man is a British army captain. Additional evidence of anti-British sentiment in New York is furnished by the advertisement reprinted above. The April 21, 1774, advertisement printed in a New York newspaper announces the arrival of a British East India Company ship carrying tea and urges the city's citizens to join in protest of British taxation.

New York was a leader in colonial opposition to the tax and lodged a formal protest with King George III. So fierce was New Yorkers' opposition to the tax that the newly appointed stamp collector for New York City resigned his post, fearing for his life. Meeting in New York, delegates from nine of the colonies declared, according to *An American Metropolis*, that "no taxes [will] be imposed on [Englishmen] but with their own consent."

In response to the Stamp Act, a radical group, the Sons of Liberty, was formed, advocating the use of force in resistance to the new tax. The first tax stamps arrived in New York on October 22, but under the threat of a Sons of Liberty riot, they were locked up under guard in a fort. On October 31, New York merchants agreed to a boycott of English goods until the act was repealed, and a committee was formed to exchange information and coordinate the resistance with the other colonies.

Two weeks of mob rule by the Sons of Liberty followed. The city's port was closed and business came to a standstill. The lieutenant-governor was burned in effigy and not a single stamp was sold. Things quieted down with the arrival of Sir Henry Moore, New York's only colonial-born governor (born in Jamaica), and his suspension of the Stamp Act on November 13.

In the face of such stiff resistance and the economic hardship to the Crown brought about by the boycott, Parliament reluctantly repealed the Stamp Act in March 1766. In celebration, a triumphant New York Assembly ordered the construction of a statue of King George III, while the Sons of Liberty erected a "liberty pole" to show their elation. The political crisis had been averted in as peaceful a manner as possible, but not before the seeds of revolt had been planted in the hearts and minds of the New York colonists.

CHAPTER 4

In the aftermath of the Stamp Act crisis, tensions between New Yorkers and the Crown remained high as Britain continued to exert its authority over the rebellious colony. In 1765, in what the colonists saw as yet another attempt at unfair taxation, Parliament ordered the city's residents to pay for the housing of the British troops occupying New York.

The Quartering and Revenue Acts

New York's assembly balked at this tax, known as the Quartering Act, but eventually bowed to official pressure and provided a building to house the troops. However, New Yorkers refused to supply the soldiers with firewood, straw for bedding, cooking pots, or rum. The Sons of Liberty once again took to the streets in protest, leading to frequent clashes with the British soldiers. Angry soldiers cut down the liberty pole, and the situation became so tense that King George declared the city to be in rebellion.

The Road to Revolution

Governor Moore was able to calm matters by convincing the assembly to vote for money to provide the troops with winter supplies. Following the successful outcome of the vote, he adjourned the assembly. But the peace that followed was an uneasy one, and the British parliament was determined to punish the colonies for their disobedience and force them to accept the mother country's authority. On June 26, Parliament passed the Revenue Act of 1767—one of a group of legislative actions

John Lamb, a radical leader of the New York Sons of Liberty, is depicted in this nineteenth-century engraving. He is addressing an anti–tea tax meeting of the Sons of Liberty in New York's City Hall. Born in New York City, Lamb was a wine merchant who became enraged by British taxation policy. He organized street protests and riots against the Stamp Act and urged colonists to threaten and harass the British officials who tried to collect the taxes. During the American Revolution, Lamb became the captain of an artillery company in the Continental army.

known as the Townshend Acts—imposing new import duties on the colonies. This was followed on July 2 by the New York Suspending Act, which disbanded the New York Assembly for disobeying the British legislature in the matter of the Quartering Act.

Colonial opposition to the Revenue Act was slow to come, but the New York Chamber of Commerce—the first organization of its kind in the world, formed by the merchant community on April 5, 1768—finally began to agitate for renewed trade boycotts against England. At the same time, the assembly, by then reinstated, again opposed the governor's request for appropriations, and fights broke out at the reconstructed liberty pole.

These tensions came to a head on January 19, 1770, when a riot broke out between the Sons of Liberty and the British troops. The Battle of Golden Hill is considered by many to be the first true battle of the Revolutionary War, coming almost two months before the more famous Boston Massacre on March 5, 1770. The aftermath of this clash led to Parliament's repeal of the Townshend Acts, except for a tax on tea, and another uneasy peace.

The New York Tea Party

On April 27, 1773, Parliament enacted the Tea Act, designed to help the financially ailing British East India Company sell its surplus of tea. While this tea was to be sold at bargain prices, many colonists believed it was actually a ploy to gain popular acceptance of the tea tax portion of the Townshend Acts that was still in effect. As a result, colonists in New York and Philadelphia turned the tea ships away from their ports, while in Charleston, the tea was left to rot on the docks.

In Boston, the reaction against the Tea Act was far stronger. On December 16, 1773, Samuel Adams and a group of men disguised as Mohawk Indians boarded three British ships docked in the city's port and dumped the ships' cargo of 342 cases of tea into the harbor. This act of rebellion became known as the Boston Tea Party. Then, on April 22, 1774, a group of New York colonists, also dressed as Mohawk Indians, held a similar "tea party" of their own, dumping eighteen boxes of British tea into New York Harbor.

Parliament punished the Massachusetts colony for its members' actions by passing a series of so-called Intolerable Acts.

In November 1773, the Association of the Sons of Liberty of New York issued a proclamation condemning the British tax on tea and urging a boycott of British tea. The document makes five resolutions for how the Sons of Liberty intend to impose a boycott on British tea. These include branding as an enemy of liberty anyone who imports British tea to the colonies; unloads and stores it; or buys, sells, or transports it. In addition, the businesses of anyone who breaks any of these resolutions would be boycotted and the individuals shunned. See transcription on page 55.

Among these was a bill to close Boston Harbor until the British East India Company was paid for the destroyed tea and Parliament received the taxes due on it. New York reacted to Britain's retaliation against Massachusetts by creating the Committee of Fifty-one on May 16, 1774. The committee became the first American organization to call for a meeting of all the colonies for the purpose of deciding a common course in their response to the Intolerable Acts and British rule in general. The First Continental Congress met in Philadelphia on September 5, 1774.

On July 6, 1776, John Hancock, president of the Continental Congress, sent a copy of the Declaration of Independence to General George Washington in New York City. On July 9, Washington read the document to his troops in New York. That night, excited and inspired by the declaration, some pro-independence New York colonists pulled down and destroyed the statue of King George III that stood at lower Manhattan's Bowling Green, on Broadway. This rebellious act is depicted in the above eighteenth-century engraving.

The Continental Congress and the Declaration of Independence

By October, the First Continental Congress had ratified the Declaration of Rights and Grievances, written by the New York delegate John Jay, the future first chief justice of the Supreme Court and governor of New York State. The Declaration of Independence stated that the colonists were "entitled to all the rights, liberties, and immunities of free and natural born subjects within the realm of England." The delegates further claimed that "the English colonists are not represented . . . in the British parliament, they are entitled

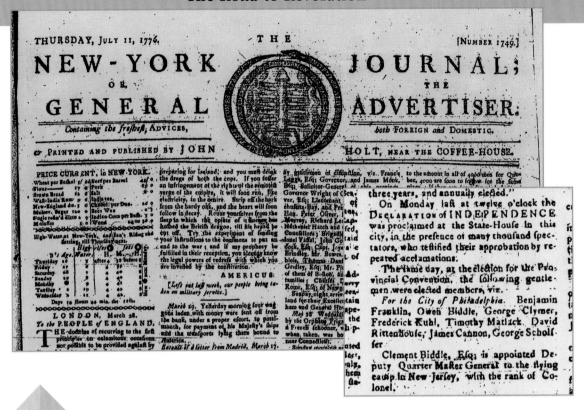

The New-York Journal, or, The General Advertiser was a New York City news-paper published by John Holt, a staunchly pro-independence New York colonist and a strong supporter of the New York Sons of Liberty. In this July 11, 1776, issue of Holt's paper, the front page includes a report on the July 8 reading of the Declaration of Independence at Philadelphia's State House (Independence Hall). The inset shows this report. During the American Revolution and the British occupation of New York City, Holt had to flee upstate but continued to publish his paper in Kingston and Poughkeepsie.

to a free and exclusive power of legislation in their several provincial legislatures, where their right of representation can alone be preserved, in all cases of taxation and internal polity, subject only to the negative of the sovereign." The colonies were all but saying that the crown had only limited sovereignty over internal politics in America and should stop trying to impose more.

The congress ordered an end to trade with Britain as New York and its sister colonies prepared for what was once unthinkable—war with the mother country. On April 23, 1775, New Yorkers learned that Bostonians had engaged in combat with British troops, leading to the radical Committee of One Hundred taking charge of New York on May 1. For their own safety, British troops were evacuated to ships in the harbor, and on August 23, the city's militiamen exchanged cannon fire with the warship *Asia*. By the end of the summer, the British governor of New York was trying to rule his rebellious province, now in the control of revolutionaries, from a British warship.

In April 1776, General George Washington, commander of the revolutionary army formed by the Continental Congress, began moving his troops into New York to protect its valuable port from British troops. On July 2, congressional delegates from twelve of the thirteen colonies voted to support the resolution for independence drafted in Philadelphia. New York, which had initially abstained, made the vote unanimous on July 9, when it endorsed the Declaration of Independence.

Citizens gathered on New York's Bowling Green to hear the reading of the Declaration of Independence. They then toppled the statue of King George III that had been erected after the repeal of the Stamp Act in 1766. The statue was later melted down to make more than 42,000 bullets for the fight for independence.

On July 11, the Declaration of Independence was published by New York's *Packet and Journal* and Annapolis's *Gazette*. New York considered itself a colony no more.

CHAPTER 5

The British made every effort to recapture Manhattan, the greatest port in America, from Washington's forces. After several battles, revolutionary troops were forced to retreat on November 16, 1776, and New York City would remain in British hands for the next seven years. It was liberated on November 25, 1783, but not before a full third of the battles of the Revolutionary War took place within the colony's borders.

Post-revolutionary New York State

On July 26, 1788, New York State, which contains New York City, became the eleventh state to be admitted into the United States of America. New York City served as the new nation's first capital from 1785 to 1790, and was the site of the inauguration of America's first president, George Washington, the former Continental army general. Though the government was to move, first to Philadelphia and then to the newly created Washington, D.C., New York was to remain an important

From America's First Capital to America's Foremost City

economic and social center of the country. It would eventually overtake Boston as America's largest city, its port the busiest in the nation. Settlements spread up the Hudson River valley and across the state. In 1825, the 363-mile-long (585 km) Erie Canal opened, linking Lake Erie with New York City. The canal opened the country west of the Appalachian Mountains to settlement by

On September 12, 1776, General George Washington gave the order for his troops to evacuate New York City in advance of a British invasion. At this time, the British had gained control of Staten Island, Long Island, and Brooklyn. On September 15, British forces landed in Manhattan, sailing into Kips Bay on the east side of the island. This event is depicted in the above nineteenth-century French engraving entitled *Debarquement des Troupes Angloises a Nouvelle Yorck, Septembre 1776* (The Landing of English Troops in New York, September 1776). The British would remain in New York until November 25, 1783, when they evacuated the city following the end of the war.

offering a cheap way to transport produce, raw materials, and natural resources (such as coal and iron) to the city and to carry manufactured goods into the Great Lakes region.

During the Civil War (1861–1865), New York provided more men and money to the Union cause than any other state. After the war, the city became a manufacturing center, leading the way in America's late nineteenth-century Industrial Revolution.

In 1894, the five separate cities of Manhattan, Brooklyn, the Bronx, Queens, and Staten Island adopted a constitution and united to form New York City. Beginning with the 1883 opening of the majestic Brooklyn Bridge, spanning the East River between Brooklyn and Manhattan, the city would be drawn even closer together through a series of bridges, highways, and public transportation systems, including the world-famous New York City subway. With the advent of the underground rapid transit system, the city's populace was free to live anywhere in the five boroughs, regardless of where they worked, leading to a population explosion in Queens, Brooklyn, and the Bronx.

Modern New York

As the home of Wall Street, the financial center of the country, New York was hard hit by the Great Depression of the 1930s, but rebounded with the rest of America. In fact, it was a New York native, Franklin Delano Roosevelt of Hyde Park, a former governor of the state, who led the country as president of the United States (1933–1945) through the worst of the Depression and World War II (1939–1945). Roosevelt was one of five New Yorkers to serve in the White House, following Martin Van Buren, a native of Kinderhook (1837–1841); Millard Fillmore, born in the Finger Lakes region (1850–1853); Grover Cleveland, raised in upstate New York (1885–1889; 1893–1897), and Theodore Roosevelt, born and raised in Manhattan (1901–1909).

The first half of the twentieth century also saw the emergence of New York City as a cultural center. Modern theater came to Broadway, and radio and television grew from novelties to major

THE GRAND DISPLAY OF FIREWORKS AND ILLUMINATIONS

After fourteen long and trouble-plagued years of construction, the Brooklyn Bridge opened to the public on May 24, 1883. More than 150,000 people crossed the bridge on opening day, as did 1,800 vehicles. Pedestrians were charged one cent to cross, while vehicles were charged five cents. The nineteenth-century color engraving that appears above commemorates this event. The opening of the bridge, which provided a quick and convenient link between Brooklyn and Manhattan, was one of the most important factors in the consolidation of the five boroughs into a single, unified city—New York City.

means of mass communication. The motion picture industry was born in New York before moving west to California. Publishing, too, took root in New York, and the city is still home to a majority of the nation's major publishers.

From its founding as a remote Dutch trading post and its leadership in the American independence movement to its current role as the commercial heart of the country, New York City and New York State have never lost their central importance to the United States. America's first city, capital of one of its most powerful and influential former colonies, continues to lead the nation toward a future of great possibilities.

TIMELINE

October 12, 1492 — Italian navigator Christopher Columbus discovers the islands of the Bahamas, Hispaniola, and Cuba, coming within 90 miles (145 km) of North America.

April 17, 1524 — Giovanni da Verrazano, an Italian explorer hired by France, sails into New York Bay to the mouth of the Hudson River.

September 1609 — English navigator Henry Hudson, working for the Dutch, explores the Hudson River as far as Albany and claims the surrounding land for the Netherlands.

1613 — Explorers Hendrick Christaensen and Adriaen Block explore the Hudson River and Long Island and name the fur trading post they leave behind New Netherland.

October 11, 1614 — The Dutch legislature grants a three-year fur-trading monopoly to the New Netherland Company.

June 3, 1621 — A new trade monopoly is granted to the Dutch West India Company. By 1625, the settlement known as New Amsterdam is established on the southern tip of Manhattan.

May 4, 1626 — New Netherland's new director, Peter Minuit, lands in New Amsterdam. He will buy the island of Manhattan from the Canarsie Indians for $24.

June 7, — The Dutch West India Company adopts the
1629　　Charter of Freedoms and Exemptions, offering
property to investors promising to settle new
colonists in New Netherland.

May 11, — Peter Stuyvesant arrives to lead New Netherland.
1647　　He will be the last Dutch governor of the colony.

1664　— Britain takes control of New Amsterdam, renaming
the territory New York.

August 8, — The Netherlands retakes New York, returning it to
1673　　British control on February 6, 1674, at the end of a
war between the two nations.

October — The British enact the Stamp Act, taxing the
19, 1765　American colonists without giving them representation in the British parliament.

June 26, — Parliament passes the first of the Intolerable Acts,
1767　　imposing taxes on colonists and limiting their
freedoms.

April 22, — New Yorkers dump British tea into New York
1774　　Harbor rather than pay controversial taxes.

July 9, — New York ratifies the Declaration of
1776　　Independence.

PRIMARY SOURCE TRANSCRIPTIONS

Page 20: Translation of a 1626 letter from Dutch West India Company administrator Peter Schaghen to the States General of the Netherlands concerning the purchase of Manhattan by New Netherland governor Peter Minuit

Transcription

High and Mighty Lords,

Yesterday the ship the Arms of Amsterdam arrived here. It sailed from New Netherland out of the River Mauritius on the 23d of September. They report that our people are in good spirit and live in peace. The women also have borne some children there. They have purchased the Island Manhattes from the Indians for the value of 60 guilders. It is 11,000 morgens in size [about 22,000 acres (8,903 hectares)]. They had all their grain sowed by the middle of May, and reaped by the middle of August. They sent samples of these summer grains: wheat, rye, barley, oats, buckwheat, canary seed, beans and flax. The cargo of the aforesaid ship is:

7246 Beaver skins
178½ Otter skins
675 Otter skins
48 Mink skins
36 Lynx skins
33 Minks
34 Muskrat skins

Many oak timbers and nut wood. Herewith, High and Mighty Lords, be commended to the mercy of the Almighty,

Your High and Mightinesses' obedient, P. Schaghen

Page 32: Translation and excerpt of the 1664 document entitled "Artykelen van't overgaen van Nieuw-Nederlandt" (Articles of Capitulation on the Reduction of New Netherland), signed on August 27, 1664

Transcription

These Articles following were consented to by the persons hereunder subscribed at the Governor's Bowry, August 27th Old Style, 1664.

1. We consent that the States-General or West India Company shall freely enjoy all farms and houses (except such as are in the forts), and that within six months they shall have free liberty to transport all such arms and ammunition as now do belong to them, or else they shall be paid for them.

2. All public houses shall continue for the uses which they are now for.

3. All people shall still continue free denizens and enjoy their lands, houses, goods, shipps, wheresoever they are within this country, and dispose of them as they please.

4. If any inhabitant have a mind to remove himself he shall have a year and six weeks from this day to remove himself, wife, children, servants, goods, and to dispose of his lands here.

5. If any officer of State, or Public Minister of State, have a mind to go for England, they shall be transported, freight free, in his Majesty's frigates, when these frigates shall return thither.

6. It is consented to, that any people may freely come from the Netherlands and plant in this country, and that Dutch vessels may freely come hither, and any of the Dutch may freely return home, or send any sort of merchandise home in vessels of their own country.

7. All ships from the Netherlands, or any other place, and goods therein, shall be received here and sent hence after the manner which formerly they were before our coming hither for six months next ensuing.

8. The Dutch here shall enjoy the liberty of their consciences in Divine Worship and church discipline.

Page 43: Excerpt of a November 1773 proclamation written by the Association of the Sons of Liberty of New York condemning the British tax on tea

Transcription
It is essential to the freedom and security of a free people, that no taxes be imposed upon them but by their own consent, or their representatives. For "What property have they in that which another may, by right, take when he

pleases to himself?" The former is the undoubted right of Englishmen, to secure which they expended millions and sacrificed the lives of thousands. And yet, to the astonishment of all the world, and the grief of America, the Commons of Great Britain, after the repeal of the memorable and detestable Stamp Act, reassumed the power of imposing taxes on the American colonies; and insisting on it as a necessary badge of parliamentary supremacy, passed a bill, in the seventh year of his present Majesty's reign, imposing duties on all glass, painters' colours, paper, and teas, that should, after the 20th of November, 1767, be "imported from Great Britain into any colony or plantation in America." This bill, after the concurrence of the Lords, obtained the royal assen . . . As this denial, and the execution of that Act, involves our slavery, and would sap the foundation of our freedom, whereby we should become slaves to our brethren and fellow subjects, born to no greater stock of freedom than the Americans—the merchants and inhabitants of this city, in conjunction with the merchants and inhabitants of the ancient American colonies, entered into an agreement to decline a part of their commerce with Great Britain, until the above mentioned Act should be totally repealed . . .

1st. Resolved, that whoever shall aid or abet, or in any manner assist, in the introduction of tea from any place whatsoever, into this colony, while it is subject, by a British Act of Parliament, to the payment of a duty, for the purpose of raising a revenue in America, he shall be deemed an enemy to the liberties of America.

2d. Resolved, that whoever shall be aiding, or assisting, in the landing, or carting of such tea, from any ship, or vessel, or shall hire any house, storehouse, or cellar or any place whatsoever, to deposit the tea, subject to a duty as aforesaid, he shall be deemed an enemy to the liberties of America.

3d. Resolved, that whoever shall sell, or buy, or in any manner contribute to the sale, or purchase of tea, subject to a duty as aforesaid, or shall aid, or abet, in transporting such tea, by land or water, from this city, until the 7th George III, chap. 46, commonly called the Revenue Act, shall be totally and clearly repealed, he shall be deemed an enemy to the liberties of America.

4th. Resolved, that whether the duties on tea, imposed by this Act, be paid in Great Britain or in America, our liberties are equally affected.

5th. Resolved, that whoever shall transgress any of these resolutions, we will not deal with, or employ, or have any connection with him.

GLOSSARY

autonomy The state of being self-governing; the right of self-government.

bastion A stronghold or fortified position.

burgher A citizen of a town; a member of the merchant class.

burgomaster The principal magistrate of a city or town, comparable to a mayor.

charter A written contract; a guarantee of rights and privileges granted by the ruling power of a state or country.

colony A body of people living in a new territory that is governed by a parent state.

constitution A document detailing the basic principles and laws of a government, its powers and duties, and the rights of its citizens.

declaration An official statement of principles.

delegate A person chosen by a group to represent them at a meeting.

economy The flow of money within a country, state, region, city, town, or household.

export To send something outside of one's country.

import To bring into one's country something from another country.

indigenous Having originated in a particular region or environment; native.

Intolerable Acts A series of laws passed by the British parliament to punish the colony of Massachusetts after the Boston Tea Party. Also known as the Coercive Acts.

legislature A lawmaking body.

monopoly Control excercised by only one company over an industry or product.

Parliament The British legislature; the part of the government that passes laws in Great Britain.

patroon The proprietor of an estate in colonial New Netherland. The patroon was granted his land under Dutch rule, but these land grants sometimes existed until the mid-nineteenth century.

repeal To take back, or cancel, a law.

sachem A chief of a North American Indian tribe or confederation, particularly an Algonquian chief.

schepen An alderman or a member of a city council.

sovereignty The power to be self-governing and independent.

tariff A tax on imported or exported goods.

Union The group of states that did not secede, or separate from, the federal government during the American Civil War. The Union (composed mostly of Northern states) was opposed by the rebellious, mostly Southern states, which formed the Confederate States of America, commonly referred to as the Confederacy. More generally, "Union" refers to the gathering or uniting of the individual states under a single federal government, creating the United States of America. Today, "the Union" is still used to refer to the United States.

FOR MORE INFORMATION

Institute for New York State Studies
Empire State Plaza
P.O. Box 2432
Albany, NY 12220-0432
Web site: http://www.nyhistory.com

Museum of the City of New York
1220 Fifth Avenue
New York, NY 10029
Web site: http://www.mcny.org

New York Historical Society
170 Central Park West
New York, NY 10024
(212) 873-3400
Web site: http://www.nyhistory.org

New York State Historical Association
P.O. Box 800
Cooperstown, NY 13326
(888) 547-1450
Web site: http://www.nysha.org/about/index.htm

Web Sites

Due to the changing nature of Internet links, the Rosen Publishing Group, Inc., has developed an online list of Web sites related to the subject of this book. This site is updated regularly. Please use this link to access the list:

http://www.rosenlinks.com/pstc/neyo

FOR FURTHER READING

Banks, Joan, and Arthur M. Schlesinger. *Peter Stuyvesant: Dutch Military Leader*. Langhorne, PA: Chelsea House Publications, 2000.

Fradin, Dennis B. *The New York Colony*. New York, NY: Children's Press, 1988.

Krizner, L. J., et al. *Peter Stuyvesant: New Amsterdam and the Origins of New York*. New York, NY: PowerPlus Books, 2002.

Lilly, Melinda, and Laura Jacobsen. *The Dutch in New Amsterdam*. Vero Beach, FL: Rourke Publishing, 2002.

Middlekauff, Robert. *The Glorious Cause: The American Revolution, 1763-1789*. New York, NY: Oxford University Press, 2005.

Morgan, Lewis Henry. *League of the Iroquois*. Sacramento, CA: Citadel Press, 1984.

Paulson, Timothy J. *New York*. New York, NY: Children's Press, 2004.

Somervill, Barbara A. *The New York Colony*. Chanhassen, MN: Child's World, 2003.

Stewart, Mark. *New York History*. Portsmouth, NH: Heinemann-Raintree, 2003.

Thornton, Jeremy. *History of Early New York*. New York, NY: PowerKids Press, 2003.

Wiener, Roberta, and James R. Arnold. *New York*. Chicago, IL: Raintree, 2004.

BIBLIOGRAPHY

Burns, Ric, et al. *New York: An Illustrated History*. New York, NY: Knopf, 2003.

Burrows, Edwin G., et al. *Gotham: A History of New York City to 1898*. New York, NY: Oxford University Press, 1998.

Ellis, David M., et al. *A Short History of New York State*. Ithaca, NY: Cornell University Press, 1957.

Jackson, Kenneth T., et al., eds. *Empire City*. New York, NY: Columbia University Press, 2002.

Klein, Milton M. *The Empire State: A History of New York*. New York, NY: Cornell University Press, 2001.

Lankevich, George. *American Metropolis: A History of New York City*. New York, NY: New York University Press, 1998.

Morris, Jan. *The Great Port: A Passage Through New York*. New York, NY: Oxford University Press, 1969.

Shorto, Russell. *The Island at the Center of the World: The Epic Story of Dutch Manhattan, the Forgotten Colony That Shaped America*. New York, NY: Doubleday, 2004.

PRIMARY SOURCE IMAGE LIST

Page 9 (right): A September 1609 diary entry from Robert Juet's journal. Housed in the Pierpont Morgan Library, New York City.

Page 10: A 1614 map by Adriaen Block of Manhattan, Long Island, and the southern New England coast.

Page 13 (top): A seventeenth-century painting by Andries van Eertvelt entitled *The Return to Amsterdam of the Fleet of the Dutch East India Company*. Housed in the Johnny van Haeften Gallery, London, England.

Page 13 (bottom): A 1621 English language printing of the *Orders and Articles Granted by the High and Mightie Lords the States General of the United Provinces, Concerning the Erecting of a West India Companie*. Printed in London, England.

Page 15: A 1651 engraving entitled *T'Fort nieuw Amsterdam op de Manhatans* (Fort New Amsterdam on Manhattan). It was published by Joost Hartgers in a 1651 book entitled *Beschrijvinghe Van Virginia, Nieuw Nederlandt, Nieuw Engelandt, En d'Eylanden Bermudes, Barbados, en S. Christoffel* (A Description of Virginia, New Netherland, New England, and the islands of Bermuda, Barbados, and St. Christoffel).

Page 18: A 1650 watercolor by Laurens Block entitled *New Amsterdam, New Netherland, 1650*. Housed in the New-York Historical Society, New York City.

Page 20 (right): A 1626 letter from Dutch West India Company administrator Peter Schaghen to the States General of the Netherlands concerning the purchase of Manhattan by New Netherland governor Peter Minuit. Housed in the Nationaal Archief van Nederland.

Page 22: A 1630 printing of the Dutch West India's Charter of Freedoms and Exceptions. Housed in the National Library of the Netherlands, The Hague, Netherlands.

Page 25 (top): A 1664 map entitled "A Description of the Towne of Mannados or New Amsterdam as it was in September 1661," also known as "The Duke's Plan of New York." Housed in the British Library, London, England.

Page 27: An oil portrait on wood panel of Peter Stuyvesant painted between 1660 and 1663, by Henri Couturier. Housed in the New-York Historical Society.

Page 32: A 1664 document entitled "Artykelen van't overgaen van Nieuw-Nederlandt" (Articles of Capitulation on the Reduction of New Netherland), signed on August 27, 1664. Housed in the National Library of the Netherlands, The Hague, Netherlands.

Page 38 (top left): A 1775 mezzotint print by Philip Dawe entitled *The patriotick barber of New York, or the Captain in the suds*. First printed in London, England, for the publishers R. Sayer & J. Bennett on February 14, 1775. Housed in the British Cartoon Collection of the Library of Congress, Washington, D.C.

Page 38 (bottom right): An April 21, 1774, advertisement printed in a New York broadside newspaper announcing the arrival of a British East India Company ship carrying tea and urging the city's citizens to join in protest of British taxation policy.

Page 41: A nineteenth-century engraving by John Karst of former New York City mayor John Lamb addressing an anti–tea tax meeting of the Sons of Liberty in New York's City Hall. Housed in the Library of Congress, Washington, D.C.

Page 43: A November 1773 proclamation written by the Association of the Sons of Liberty of New York condemning the British tax on tea and urging a boycott of British tea.

Page 44: An eighteenth-century engraving entitled *Le destruction de la statue royale a Nouvelle Yorck* (The Destruction of the Royal Statue in New York), by Johannes Adam Simon Oertel. First published in Paris, France. Housed in the New-York Historical Society.

Page 45: The July 11, 1776 issue of the *New-York Journal, or, The General Advertiser*, published by John Holt in New York City.

Page 48: A nineteenth-century French engraving entitled *Debarquement des Troupes Angloises a Nouvelle Yorck, Septembre 1776* (The Landing of English Troops in New York, September 1776). First published by J. Chereau in Paris France.

Page 50: A nineteenth-century color engraving entitled *Bird's-Eye View of the Great New York and Brooklyn Bridge and the Grand Display of Fireworks on Opening Night in 1883*. Housed in the New-York Historical Society.

INDEX

A

Adams, Samuel, 42
Algonquian Indians, 4
Andros, Edmund, 34-35, 36
Anglo-Dutch War, 31

B

Battle of Golden Hill, 42
Bolting Act, 35, 36
Boston Massacre, 42
Boston Tea Party, 42
British East India Company, 42, 43
Bronck, Jonas, 23-24
Bronx, 33, 49
    origin of name, 23-24
Brooklyn, 8, 11, 14, 23, 49

C

Charles II, King (Britain), 28, 36
Charter of Freedoms and Exemptions, 21
Columbus, Christopher, 6-7
Committee of Fifty-one, 43
Committee of One Hundred, 46
Continental Congress, 43, 44-46

D

Declaration of Independence, 44-46
Dutch East India Company, 9-11, 14
Dutch West India Company, 12-16, 18, 21,
    22, 28
    complaints against, 26
    interest in New Netherland, 17

F

fur trade, 12, 15, 17, 21, 22, 23

G

George II, King (Britain), 30
George III, King (Britain), 39, 40, 46

H

Harlem, 33
Hiawatha, 5-6
Hudson, Henry, 8-16

I

Indians/Native Americans, 4-7, 11, 15, 19-21,
    23, 24, 42
Intolerable Acts, 42-43

J

James, Duke of York/King James II, 29-30, 31,
    35, 36
Jay, John, 44

K

Kieft, Willem, 23-24, 26, 27
Krol, Bastiaen Jansean, 22-23

L

League of Five Nations, 5
Long Island, 4, 5, 11, 12, 21, 23, 26, 28, 31, 36

M

Mahican Indians, 7
Manhattan, 5, 11, 12, 14, 23, 24, 31, 33, 35, 49
    origin of name, 4
    purchase of, 18-22
    Revolutionary War and, 47
Minuit, Peter, 18-19, 22
Mohawk Indians, 6, 28, 42
Mohican/Muhhekunneuw Indians, 4

N

Netherlands, the, 12, 14, 17, 21, 22, 23
    reoccupation of New York, 34
    war with Britain, 31, 33
New Amsterdam, 16, 17, 18,
    British conquer of, 28-30
    government of, 26-30
    settlement of, 14, 24
New Jersey, 23, 33, 36
New Netherland, 12, 15, 17, 18, 23, 24
    British conquer of, 28-30
    government of, 26-30
    settlement of, 21
New York,
    early government of, 31, 35-37
    first British governor of, 31

first elections in, 35
first mayor of, 33
New York City, 35, 47, 49–51
New York Tea Party, 42–43
Nicolls, Richard, 31–33

Q
Quartering Act, 40–41

R
Revenue Act, 40–41

S
slaves, 7
Sons of Liberty, 39, 40, 42
Stamp Act, 37–39, 40, 46

Staten Island, 8, 24, 33, 49
origin of name, 21
Suspending Act, 41
Stuyvesant, Peter, 26, 27, 28, 30, 31

T
Tea Act, 42
Townshend Acts, 41, 42

V
Verrazano, Giovanni da, 8, 16

W
Wall Street, 24, 49
Washington, George, 46, 47
William, King (Britain), 36

About the Author

Paul Kupperberg is a writer, full-time editor, and native New Yorker. He has written numerous history and science books for the Rosen Publishing Group, including ones on such topics as the R.M.S. *Titanic*, spy satellites, astronauts, the Great Depression, disease, and Edwin Hubble and the big bang. Kupperberg is a keen student of history and has a particular interest in the history of his hometown—New York City.

Photo Credits

Cover, p. 1, © New-York Historical Society, New York, USA/Bridgeman Art Library; p. 5 © North Wind/North Wind Archives; p. 9 (left), 13 (top), 13 (bottom), 20 (bottom), 29, 30, 41, © Bettmann/Corbis; p. 9 (right) © The Pierpont-Morgan Library/Art Resource, NY; p. 10 Courtesy of Willem Rabbeljee, Enschede, the Netherlands; p. 13 (top) Johnny Van Haeften Gallery, London, UK /Bridgeman Art Library; pp. 15, 20 (inset), 25 (inset) © Corbis; pp. 18, 34 © Museum of the City of New York, USA/Bridgeman Art Library; p. 19 © Len Tantillo; pp. 20 (top), 22, 32 Koninklijke Bibliotheek/National Library of the Netherlands and Het Geheugan van Nederland/Memory of the Netherlands; p. 25 (top) © British Library, London, UK/Bridgeman Art Library; p. 27 © Stapleton Collection/Corbis; pp. 37, 39, 44, 50 Library of Congress Prints and Photographs Division; p. 38 (inset) New-York Historical Society; p. 41 Library of Congress, Washington, D.C., USA/Bridgeman Art Library; p. 43 © Getty Images; p. 45 Courtesy of the New York Public Library; p. 48 © Private Collection/Bridgeman Art Library.

Photo Researcher: Hillary Arnold